INTIMATE RELATIONS

Intimate Relations
or Sixty Years a Bastard

T. E. B. CLARKE

LONDON
MICHAEL JOSEPH

First published in Great Britain by
MICHAEL JOSEPH LTD
52 Bedford Square
London, W.C.1.
1971

7181 0927 9

Filmset in 12pt Bembo
by Filmtype Services Ltd,
printed by Hollen Street Press Ltd
on paper supplied by P. F. Bingham Ltd and
bound by James Burn at Esher, Surrey

My name is Henry Bates. I was
born in the year 1880 –

– near the Yorkshire
village of Rudery. My
mother had been a
nursemaid at Rudery Hall,
ancient seat of the Earls of
Flushwater.

Here she found favour in the eyes of her employer, Viscount Firkin, the old Earl's heir.

Eventually the poor woman realised that she could not conceal her condition any longer.

She confessed her shame, and was driven out by her coldhearted mistress.

My mother sought sanctuary from the elements in a rude stone hovel on the moors which was quaintly termed by the local inhabitants "t'owd squat 'ole."

Here, in the following summer,
her child was delivered.

As soon as he heard the news my father, an honourable
man, sent word for my mother to bring me to Rudery
Hall –

– where I quickly became the favourite of all the little victims of Viscount Firkin's local indiscretions.

I never saw my mother again. Later I learned that my father had paid her passage to one of our colonies.

9

Life at Rudery Hall offered
many delights to the growing
child.

Each youngster was allowed a pet
of his or her own. My
half-brother, the Hon. Eustace
Plugg, kept a stinkeroo –

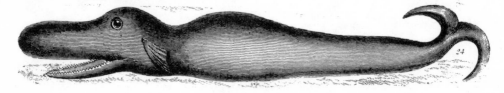

– and my half-sister, the Hon.
Pompilia Plugg, had a tame
dirtibeeste –

– but the presence of such creatures in the house was,
I am afraid, occasionally resented by old Slapcock,
the butler.

My chief companions were my half-brother, Eustace,
from whom I learned the facts of life –

– little Annie Tumble, the coachman's daughter, who helped me to test the accuracy of Eustace's information –

– and my grandfather, the fourteenth Earl, who had just entered his second childhood.

13

The old Earl's mind had been failing for some time. He had taken to having breakfast with his horse.

– and often he would sit for hours gazing sadly at his cock.

He had also formed the strange habit of crawling into haystacks

14

– not always, I fear, from the
most innocent of motives.

He had developed a regrettable
tendency to play Peeping
Tom –

– and once he was nearly arrested
for exposing his female to a
person.

15

The rest of the family were, in many respects, highly talented.

The Hon. Wilhelmina Plugg will be remembered for her recitals at the Aeolian Hall

– and the Hon. Cordelia ("Aunt Smelly") was famous for her pianoforte duets with my Uncle Egbert.

Lady Pearl Flushwater was
probably the county's best
all-round sportswoman

My cousin Rowena was an old
Oxford oar

– and my Aunt Flavia was
considered the most promising
middle-weight in the West
Riding.

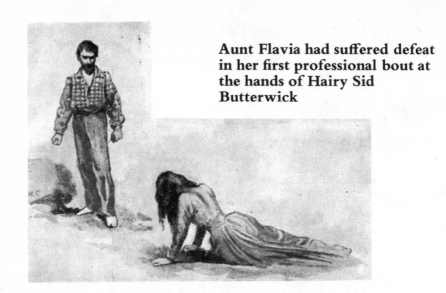

Aunt Flavia had suffered defeat in her first professional bout at the hands of Hairy Sid Butterwick

– but she made such a good come-back against Streaky O'Halloran, the Fighting Grocer of Huddersfield –

– that we matched her with the Dixie Kid.

My aunt delighted us all by reducing the Negro to impotence in eight smashing rounds.

But my chief hero in those early days was my brilliant Uncle Roland, who had been acclaimed the most progressive designer of water-closets in the land.

He it was who designed the Roland Plugg water-closet for use in tramcars.

He was also the first man to equip a bicycle with a water-closet –

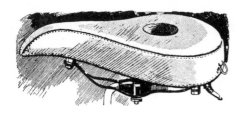

– which, with the addition of a special saddle, could be used without the need to dismount –

– and before his thirtieth year he had invented a means whereby water-closets in railway trains could be used while they were standing in stations.

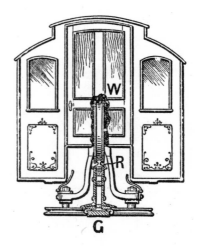

21

I also had a certain sense of affection – born mainly,
I think, of pity – for my Uncle Hector.

Poor man, it was his affliction to
be incapable of controlling his
wind –

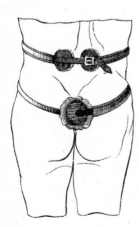

– although he had tried every
known preventive –

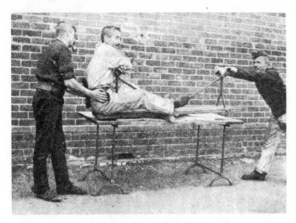

– and had received the best
medical attention.

My uncle's unfortunate disability
caused him shame and
embarrassment wherever he
went.

23

Once he was even ejected
from the smoking-room
of his club.

And never shall I forget
what happened on the day
Uncle Hector went
bathing at Clacton.

I am told that he had to propose
to Aunt Maud from a distance of
twenty yards –

– and she accepted him only on
condition that he gave her, as
his wedding present, a chair
fitted with an automatic fan.

Of my Uncle Algie I saw little. Uncle A. was the black sheep of the family.

He used to behave coarsely in
the company of ladies –

– and his conduct became intolerable when he insulted our neighbour, Lady Pamela Whiddle.

My uncle had his own version of this incident. He maintained that all he did was to pull out the end of his shirt and exclaim jocularly: "Twelve and six with two collars. Not bad, eh?"

27

However, it resulted in Uncle Algie leaving Rudery under a cloud. He betook himself to France –

– where he got into trouble with the authorities for stealing the front wheel of a gendarme's bicycle –

– and, when interrogated, spitting at the local Prefet down the telephone.

He was arrested and sentenced
to seven years' penal servitude.

We thought that was the end of
Uncle Algie – but no! Every few
weeks he would ring up from
Devil's Island to ask for money.
He was a bad lot.

"Queer" is the only adjective that will describe my Uncle Sylvester.

He used to walk about with a lady's handbag on his arm.

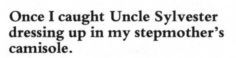

Once I caught Uncle Sylvester dressing up in my stepmother's camisole.

He kept the <u>oddest</u> manservant –

– and he had an equally queer circle of friends.

There was one relative whom we children were
forbidden to meet. He lived in the West Tower,
the door of which defied all our efforts to open it

– until one day Eustace and I
found that it had been
accidentally left unlocked.
We burst in, and with something
of a shock –

– found ourselves being warmly
greeted by the Flushwater
Monster!

33

My education was placed in the
capable hands – five, to be
exact – of the Rev. Theodore
Weech.

He saw to it that I made an early
start in the acquirement of
useful knowledge.

Great was my grief when, my schooling completed, the Rev. Weech sailed to take up an appointment abroad in the ill-fated "Waratah" –

– and went down with all hands.

When I was sixteen I rode to hounds for the first time.

The pack met at Rudery Hall, and the gentlefolk rode in from all parts of the county.

Lord Eric Ponce came all the way from Piddle-in-the Marsh.

The beautiful Iris Bedworthy rode over from Tickle Slapton.

And Lady Elizabeth Rogers arrived from Fallick Towers. She, too, had never ridden before, and great was the amusement of the company when we found that she had covered the whole distance sitting backwards!

The day was marred by a most distressing accident to my half-brother Eustace.

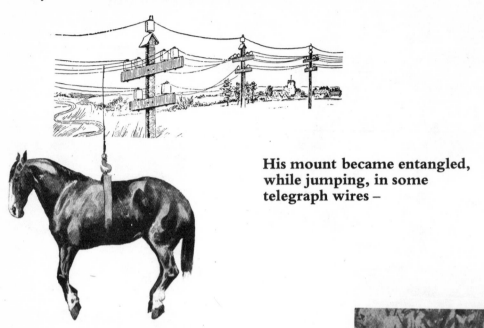

His mount became entangled, while jumping, in some telegraph wires –

– causing him to fall heavily on his head.

Poor Eustace was never quite right in his mind thereafter. He developed a strange mental aberration.

This took the form of a constant urge to commit a nuisance in visitors' hats –

– not unnaturally, to their great indignation.

**The sight of hats on the hall
table was irresistible to Eustace –**

**– and the family had to keep a
careful watch on him.**

**Once the Prime Minister honoured Rudery Hall
with a visit**

**– but even his hat was not
immune from Eustace**

**– and the great man left in high
dudgeon, despite my
stepmother's tearful apologies.**

41

Eustace would adopt the most cunning strategies in order to satisfy his urge.

Sometimes he would even set a visitor's hat on fire so that he could plead the necessity to extinguish it.

42

Eventually those who knew us
were careful never to part from
their hats when invited to
dinner.

At the age of twenty-one I fell in love with our
near neighbour, Lady Angeline Whiddle.

I made it plain that I had little
to offer her, but Angeline agreed
nevertheless to be mine.

And then – ah, sorry day! – she caught me writing a rude word on the dining-room wall, and her gentle soul was shocked.

I knew that I had lost her, and as night was falling I left Rudery to seek forgetfulness.

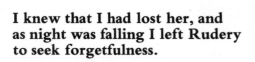

For five years I roamed the world.

I experienced the rigours of life
before the mast.

I suffered storm and
shipwreck.

I defied the laws of man
and nature.

I crossed the trackless desert.

I forded mighty rivers.

And in the end – I came back
to my childhood home.

Life, I found, had changed but little at Rudery Hall during my absence.

Old Slapcock had died, and the new butler was a surly fellow named Sorehead.

But my father, Viscount Firkin, was still engaged in his favourite pastime

– and so was Uncle Sylvester

– their activities being a source
of constant interest to the old
Earl of Flushwater.

**Uncle Hector's old complaint
was still causing Aunt Maud
some embarrassment.**

He had eased her lot considerably, however, by making thoughtful use of large leaves when conversing in the open –

– and for the comfort of others he now took his own fan with him to social events.

51

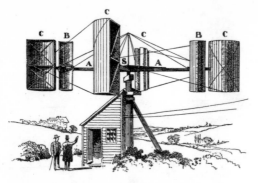

My brilliant Uncle Roland had
meanwhile designed a
water-closet with sails, for the
specific purpose of harnessing
Uncle Hector's wind.

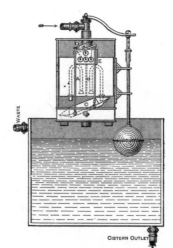

His scheme was, I fear, too
grandiose. Uncle Roland had to
abandon it when he found that
twelve men were required to
pull the plug.

This was his one failure, and it weighed heavily on my uncle's mind during his declining years.

Often we would find him peering into cisterns in the middle of the night, striving always to discover where his plans had gone amiss.

And all day he would sit silently brooding, his old hands clutching pathetically at a chain which existed only in his imagination.

Aunt Flavia, on the other hand, realised her most cherished ambition.

My aunt won the middle-weight championship from Big Joe Pizzacotti by a K.O. in the fourteenth round.

But unfortunately the mighty punch that gained her the title had wrought irremediable damage to Aunt Flavia's famed right hand.

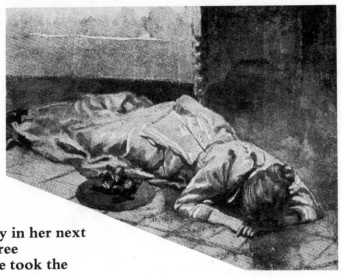

It let her down badly in her next contest, and after three punishing rounds she took the full count.

My aunt never came back. Sad, embittered, soon forgotten by the fickle public, she sought the solace of all too many broken pugilists.

Tragic also is the ending to the tale of my half-brother, Eustace.

His aberration became steadily worse. No longer was he satisfied to misuse one visitor's hat at a time: he would now collect them by the armful

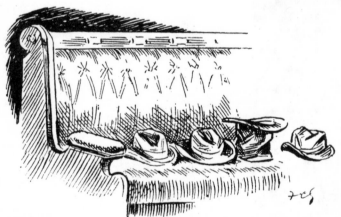

— and leave them in a deplorable condition.

He had even taught his pet rabbit, Trilby, to emulate his disgusting practice.

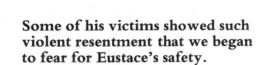

Some of his victims showed such violent resentment that we began to fear for Eustace's safety.

Our misgivings were justified. Came the fateful day
when Eustace went too far.

He committed a nuisance in the
hat of the hot-tempered Comte
de Merde

– who, on discovering the
enormity –

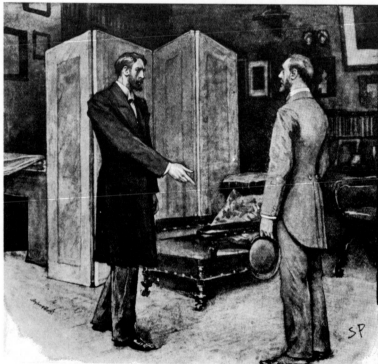

58

– drew out his pistol and
discharged it at my unfortunate
half–brother

– with the result that poor
Eustace was bedridden for the
remainder of his life.